Incredibly Easy
Grilling

Publications International, Ltd.

Favorite Brand Name Recipes at www.fbnr.com

Microwave Cooking: Microwave ovens vary in wattage. Use the cooking times as guidelines and check for doneness before adding more time.

Preparation/Cooking Times: Preparation times are based on the approximate amount of time required to assemble the recipe before cooking, baking, chilling or serving. These times include preparation steps such as measuring, chopping and mixing. The fact that some preparations and cooking can be done simultaneously is taken into account. Preparation of optional ingredients and serving suggestions is not included.

Contents

The All American Burger (p. 6)

Australian Lamb Burger
with Goat Cheese (p. 16)

Classic California Burger (p. 28)   Ranch Burger (p. 24)

Burger **Bliss**

The All-American Burger

Burger Spread (recipe follows)
1½ **pounds ground beef**
  2 **tablespoons chopped fresh parsley**
  2 **teaspoons onion powder**
  2 **teaspoons Worcestershire sauce**
  1 **teaspoon garlic powder**
  1 **teaspoon salt**
  1 **teaspoon black pepper**
  4 **hamburger buns, split**

1. Prepare Burger Spread; set aside.

2. Prepare grill for direct cooking.

3. Combine beef, parsley, onion powder, Worcestershire sauce, garlic powder, salt and pepper in medium bowl; mix lightly but thoroughly. Shape mixture into four ½-inch-thick burgers.

4. Place burgers on grid. Grill, covered, over medium heat 8 to 10 minutes (or, uncovered, 13 to 15 minutes) to medium (160°F) or to desired doneness, turning halfway through grilling time.

5. Remove burgers from grill. Place burgers between buns; top each burger with Burger Spread. *Makes 4 servings*

Burger Spread

½ **cup ketchup**
¼ **cup prepared mustard**
2 **tablespoons chopped onion**
1 **tablespoon relish or chopped pickles**
1 **tablespoon chopped fresh parsley**

Combine all ingredients in small bowl; mix well. *Makes 1 cup*

Grilled Salsa Turkey Burger

3 ounces ground turkey
1 tablespoon mild or medium salsa
1 tablespoon crushed tortilla chips
1 Monterey Jack cheese slice (optional)
1 whole wheat hamburger bun, split
1 lettuce leaf
 Additional salsa

1. Combine turkey, 1 tablespoon salsa and chips in small bowl; shape into patty. Lightly oil grid or broiler rack to prevent sticking.

2. Grill over medium-hot coals or broil 4 to 6 inches from heat 6 minutes on each side or until cooked through (160°F), turning once. Top with cheese during last 2 minutes of grilling time, if desired. Place bun, cut sides down, on grill during last 2 minutes of grilling time to toast until lightly browned.

3. Cover bottom half of bun with lettuce; top with burger, additional salsa and top half of bun. *Makes 1 serving*

Sizzlin' Burgers

Prep Time: 5 minutes • Cook Time: 15 minutes

1 pound ground beef
¼ cup *French's®* **Worcestershire Sauce**
½ teaspoon garlic salt

1. Combine ground beef, Worcestershire and garlic salt; shape into 4 burgers.

2. Grill over medium heat for 15 minutes or until no longer pink in center (160°F), turning once.

3. Serve burgers on rolls. Splash on more Worcestershire to taste.
Makes 4 servings

Blue Cheese Burgers with Red Onion

2 pounds ground beef chuck
2 cloves garlic, minced
1 teaspoon salt
½ teaspoon black pepper
4 ounces blue cheese
⅓ cup coarsely chopped walnuts, toasted
1 torpedo (long) red onion *or* 2 small red onions, sliced into
⅜-inch-thick rounds
2 baguettes (each 12 inches long)
Olive or vegetable oil

Combine beef, garlic, salt and pepper in medium bowl. Shape meat mixture into 12 oval patties. Mash cheese and blend with walnuts in small bowl. Divide cheese mixture equally; place on centers of 6 meat patties. Top with remaining meat patties; tightly pinch edges together to seal in filling.

Oil hot grid to help prevent sticking. Grill patties and onion, if desired, on covered grill, over medium KINGSFORD® Briquets, 7 to 12 minutes for medium doneness (160°F), turning once. Cut baguettes into 4-inch lengths; split each piece and brush cut side with olive oil. Move cooked burgers to edge of grill to keep warm. Grill bread, oil side down, until lightly toasted. Serve burgers on toasted baguettes.   *Makes 6 servings*

Hawaiian-Style Burgers

1½ **pounds ground beef**
⅓ **cup chopped green onions**
2 **tablespoons Worcestershire sauce**
⅛ **teaspoon black pepper**
⅓ **cup pineapple preserves**
⅓ **cup barbecue sauce**
6 **pineapple slices**
6 **hamburger buns, split and toasted**

1. Prepare grill for direct cooking. Combine beef, onions, Worcestershire and pepper in large bowl. Shape into six ½-inch-thick patties.

2. Combine preserves and barbecue sauce in small saucepan. Bring to a boil over medium heat, stirring often.

3. Place patties on grid over medium coals. Grill, covered, 8 to 10 minutes (or, uncovered, 13 to 15 minutes) to medium doneness (160°F), turning and brushing often with sauce. Place pineapple on grill; grill 1 minute or until browned, turning once.

4. To serve, place patties on buns with pineapple.   *Makes 6 servings*

Broiling Directions: Arrange patties on rack in broiler pan. Broil 4 inches from heat to medium doneness (160°F), turning and brushing often with sauce. Broil pineapple 1 minute, turning once.

Lipton® Onion Burgers

Prep Time: 10 minutes • **Cook Time:** 12 minutes

1 envelope LIPTON® RECIPE SECRETS® Onion Soup Mix*
2 pounds ground beef
½ cup water

*Also terrific with LIPTON® RECIPE SECRETS® Beefy Onion, Onion Mushroom, Beefy Mushroom, Savory Herb with Garlic or Ranch Soup Mix.

1. In large bowl, combine all ingredients; shape into 8 patties.

2. Grill or broil until done (160°F). *Makes 8 servings*

Mushroom-Stuffed Pork Burgers

¾ cup thinly sliced fresh mushrooms
¼ cup thinly sliced green onion
1 clove garlic, minced
2 teaspoons butter or margarine
1½ pounds lean ground pork
1 teaspoon Dijon-style mustard
1 teaspoon Worcestershire sauce
¼ teaspoon salt
⅛ teaspoon freshly ground pepper
6 hamburger buns (optional)

In skillet, sauté mushrooms, onion and garlic in butter until tender, about 2 minutes; set aside. Combine ground pork, mustard, Worcestershire sauce, salt and pepper; mix well. Shape into 12 patties, about 4 inches in diameter. Spoon mushroom mixture onto center of 6 patties. Spread to within ½ inch of edges. Top with remaining 6 patties; seal edges.

Place patties on grill about 6 inches over medium coals. Grill 10 to 15 minutes or until no longer pink in center (160°F), turning once. Serve on buns, if desired. *Makes 6 servings*

Favorite recipe from **National Pork Board**

Australian Lamb Burger with Goat Cheese

Prep Time: 15 minutes • **Cook Time:** 15 minutes

Burger
   1¾ **pounds ground Australian Lamb**
   1 **shallot, peeled and chopped**
   1 **tablespoon capers, chopped**
   6 to 8 **large basil leaves, sliced**
      Freshly ground pepper, to taste
   ½ **cup cornmeal (or flour), for coating**
      Olive oil, for cooking

Tomato Relish
   3 **vine-ripened tomatoes, halved crosswise**
   1 **red onion, thickly sliced**
   1 **teaspoon sugar**
   1 **teaspoon balsamic vinegar**
      Salt and freshly ground pepper, to taste

Presentation
   4 **Kaiser rolls or hamburger buns, split**
   4 **tablespoons soft goat cheese (or chèvre)**

1. To make burgers, combine ground lamb, shallot, capers, basil and pepper in a large bowl and mix well. Divide mixture into 4 burgers. Spread cornmeal over a plate and press burgers into cornmeal to coat.

2. Preheat barbecue grill or grill pan and brush with oil. Cook burgers over medium to high heat for 6-7 minutes or until internal temperature reaches 160° F.

3. To make relish, place tomatoes flesh-side down on the grill and flip after 20 seconds, cooking until skin starts to char. Grill onions until soft. Transfer to a plate and, when cool enough to handle, dice finely. Place in a bowl, add sugar and vinegar, season to taste with salt and pepper and mix well. Grill buns, cut side down, until lightly toasted. Spread with goat cheese and top with burgers. Serve with tomato relish.

Makes 4 burgers

Favorite recipe from **Meat and Livestock Australia**

Wisconsin Cheese Stuffed Burgers

3 pounds ground beef
½ cup dry bread crumbs
2 eggs
1¼ cups (5 ounces) of your favorite shredded Wisconsin cheese, shredded Pepper Havarti cheese, crumbled Blue cheese or crumbled Basil & Tomato Feta cheese

In a large mixing bowl, combine beef, bread crumbs and eggs; mix well, but lightly. Divide mixture into 24 balls; flatten each on waxed paper to 4 inches across. Place 1 tablespoon cheese on each of 12 patties. Top with remaining patties, carefully pressing edges to seal. Grill patties 4 inches from coals, turning only once, 6 to 9 minutes on each side or until cooked through (160°F). To keep cheese between patties as it melts, do not flatten burgers with spatula while grilling. *Makes 12 servings*

CAUTION: Cheese filling may be very hot if eaten immediately after cooking.

Favorite recipe from **Wisconsin Milk Marketing Board**

Southwest Pesto Burgers

Cilantro Pesto
> 1 large clove garlic
> 4 ounces fresh cilantro, tough stems removed
> 1½ teaspoons minced jalapeño pepper*
> ¼ teaspoon salt
> ¼ cup vegetable oil

Burgers
> 1¼ pounds ground beef
> ¼ cup plus 1 tablespoon Cilantro Pesto, divided
> ½ teaspoon salt
> 4 slices pepper Jack cheese
> 2 tablespoons mayonnaise
> 4 kaiser rolls, split
> 1 ripe avocado, peeled and sliced
> Salsa

Jalapeño peppers can sting and irritate the skin, so wear rubber gloves when handling peppers and do not touch your eyes.

1. For pesto, with motor running, drop garlic through feed tube of food processor; process until minced. Add cilantro, jalapeño pepper and salt; process until cilantro is chopped.

2. With motor running, slowly add oil through feed tube; process until thick paste forms. Transfer to container with tight-fitting lid. Refrigerate until needed.

3. Prepare grill for direct cooking.

4. Combine beef, ¼ cup pesto and salt in large bowl; mix well. Form into 4 patties. Place patties on grid over medium heat. Grill, covered, 8 to 10 minutes (or, uncovered, 13 to 15 minutes) to medium (160°F), turning once. Add cheese to patties during last 1 minute of grilling.

5. While patties are cooking, combine mayonnaise and remaining 1 tablespoon pesto in small bowl; mix well. Top patties with mayonnaise mixture. Serve on rolls with avocado and salsa.   *Makes 4 servings*

Serving Suggestion: Serve with refried beans.

All-American Turkey Burgers

1 pound ground turkey
½ cup chopped onion
¼ cup ketchup
1 clove garlic, minced
⅛ teaspoon pepper
4 kaiser rolls, sliced
4 leaves lettuce
4 slices tomato
4 slices onion

1. Preheat charcoal grill for direct-heat cooking.

2. In medium bowl combine turkey, onion, ketchup, garlic and pepper. Shape turkey mixture into 4 burgers, approximately 3½ inches in diameter.

3. Grill burgers 5 to 6 minutes per side until 165°F is reached on meat thermometer and meat is no longer pink in center.

4. To serve, place each burger on bottom half of roll; top with lettuce, tomato and onion and top half of roll. *Makes 4 servings*

Favorite recipe from **National Turkey Federation**

Chutney Turkey Burgers

1 pound ground turkey
½ cup purchased chutney, divided
½ teaspoon salt
½ teaspoon pepper
⅛ teaspoon hot pepper sauce
½ cup nonfat plain yogurt
1 teaspoon curry powder
4 hamburger buns, split

1. Preheat charcoal grill for direct-heat cooking.

2. In medium bowl combine turkey, ¼ cup chutney, salt, pepper and hot pepper sauce. Shape turkey mixture into 4 burgers, approximately 3½ inches in diameter. Grill turkey burgers 5 to 6 minutes per side until 165°F is reached on meat thermometer and turkey is no longer pink in center.

3. In small bowl combine yogurt, curry powder and remaining ¼ cup chutney.

4. To serve, place burgers on bottom halves of buns; spoon yogurt mixture over burgers and cover with top halves of buns.

Makes 4 servings

Favorite recipe from **National Turkey Federation**

Ranch
Burgers

1¼ pounds lean ground beef
¾ cup HIDDEN VALLEY® The Original Ranch® Salad Dressing
¾ cup dry bread crumbs
¼ cup minced onion
1 teaspoon salt
¼ teaspoon black pepper
Sesame seed buns
Lettuce, tomato slices and red onion slices (optional)
Additional HIDDEN VALLEY® The Original Ranch® Salad Dressing

In large bowl, combine beef, salad dressing, bread crumbs, onion, salt and pepper. Shape into 6 patties. Grill over medium-hot coals 5 to 6 minutes until no longer pink in center (160°F). Place on sesame seed buns with lettuce, tomato and red onion slices, if desired. Serve with a generous amount of additional salad dressing. *Makes 6 servings*

Bacon Burgers

1 pound lean ground beef
4 crisply cooked bacon slices, crumbled
1½ teaspoons chopped fresh thyme *or* ½ teaspoon dried thyme
½ teaspoon salt
Dash black pepper
4 slices Swiss cheese

1. Prepare grill for direct cooking.

2. Combine ground beef, bacon, thyme, salt and pepper in medium bowl; mix lightly. Shape into four patties.

3. Place patties on grid over medium heat. Grill, covered, 8 to 10 minutes (or, uncovered, 13 to 15 minutes) to medium (160°F) or to desired doneness, turning halfway through grilling time. Top with cheese during last 2 minutes of grilling time. *Makes 4 servings*

Easy Salmon Burgers with Honey Barbecue Sauce

⅓ **cup honey**
⅓ **cup ketchup**
1½ **teaspoons cider vinegar**
 1 **teaspoon prepared horseradish**
¼ **teaspoon minced garlic**
⅛ **teaspoon crushed red pepper flakes (optional)**
 1 **can (7½ ounces) salmon, drained**
½ **cup dried bread crumbs**
¼ **cup chopped onion**
 3 **tablespoons chopped green bell pepper**
 1 **egg white**
 2 **hamburger buns, toasted**

In small bowl, combine honey, ketchup, vinegar, horseradish, garlic and red pepper flakes until well blended. Set aside half of sauce. In separate bowl, mix together salmon, bread crumbs, onion, green pepper and egg white. Blend in 2 tablespoons remaining sauce. Divide salmon mixture into 2 patties, ½ to ¾ inch thick. Place patties on well-oiled grill, 4 to 6 inches from hot coals. Grill, turning 2 to 3 times and basting with remaining sauce, until burgers are browned and cooked through. Or place patties on lightly greased baking sheet. Broil 4 to 6 inches from heat source, turning 2 to 3 times and basting with remaining sauce, until cooked through. Place on hamburger buns and serve with reserved sauce.

Makes 2 servings

Favorite recipe from **National Honey Board**

Classic California Burger

Prep Time: 10 minutes • **Cook Time:** 10 minutes

2 tablespoons *French's*® **Honey Dijon Mustard**
2 tablespoons *French's*® *Gourmayo*™ **Caesar Ranch Mayonnaise**
2 tablespoons sour cream
1 pound ground beef
2 tablespoons *French's*® **Worcestershire Sauce**
1⅓ cups *French's*® **Cheddar or Original French Fried Onions, divided**
½ teaspoon garlic salt
¼ teaspoon ground black pepper
4 hamburger rolls, split and toasted
½ small avocado, sliced
½ cup sprouts

1. Combine mustard, mayonnaise and sour cream; set aside.

2. Combine beef, Worcestershire, ⅔ cup French Fried Onions and seasonings. Form into 4 patties. Grill over high heat until juices run clear (160°F internal temperature).

3. Place burgers on rolls. Top each with mustard sauce, avocado slices, sprouts and remaining onions, dividing evenly. Cover with top half of rolls.

Makes 4 servings

BBQ Cheese Burger: Top each burger with 1 slice American cheese, 1 tablespoon **CATTLEMEN'S**® Authentic Smoke House Barbecue Sauce and 2 tablespoons French Fried Onions.

Pizza Burger: Top each burger with pizza sauce, mozzarella cheese and French Fried Onions.

Grilled Pork Tenderloin Medallions (p. 44)

Lamb Chops with Cranberry-Orange Salsa (p. 46)

Rosemary Steak (p. 36)

Five-Spice Australian Lamb
Shoulder Chops (p. 34)

Mighty Meaty

Jamaican Steak

2 pounds beef flank steak
¼ cup packed brown sugar
3 tablespoons orange juice
3 tablespoons lime juice
3 cloves garlic, minced
1 piece (1½×1 inches) fresh ginger, minced
2 teaspoons grated orange peel
2 teaspoons grated lime peel
1 teaspoon salt
1 teaspoon black pepper
¼ teaspoon ground cinnamon
⅛ teaspoon ground cloves
   Shredded orange peel
   Shredded lime peel

Score both sides of beef.* Combine sugar, juices, garlic, ginger, grated peels, salt, pepper, cinnamon and cloves in 2-quart glass dish. Add beef; turn to coat. Cover and refrigerate steak at least 2 hours. Remove beef from marinade; discard marinade. Grill beef over medium-hot KINGSFORD® Briquets about 6 minutes per side until medium-rare (140°F) or to desired doneness. Garnish with shredded orange and lime peels.

Makes 6 servings

To score flank steak, cut ¼-inch-deep diagonal lines about 1 inch apart in surface of steak to form diamond-shaped design.

Five-Spice Australian Lamb Shoulder Chops

Marinate Time: 20 minutes or overnight • **Prep Time:** 20 minutes
Cook Time: 10 minutes

Chops & Marinade
   8 Australian Lamb shoulder chops, trimmed
   2 tablespoons red wine
   1 tablespoon honey
   1 tablespoon soy sauce
   1 teaspoon Chinese 5-spice powder*

Salad
   1 ruby red grapefruit, segmented and pith removed
   1 small bulb fennel, white part only, finely sliced
   ½ bunch cilantro, chopped
   1 bunch watercress
   1 tablespoon olive oil
   1 tablespoon lemon juice
   Sea salt and freshly ground pepper, to taste

Serve
   Loaf of sourdough bread (optional)

*Chinese 5-spice powder is available in the spice section of most supermarkets. It is usually a blend of anise, cinnamon, star anise, cloves and ginger.

1. Place the lamb chops in a flat dish. Combine the wine, honey, soy sauce and 5-spice powder and mix well. Pour over the chops, turning chops so they are fully coated in mixture. Cover and marinate 20 minutes or overnight.

2. To make the salad, combine the grapefruit, fennel, watercress and cilantro in a bowl. Whisk together the oil and juice, season with salt and pepper to taste, and toss with the salad.

3. Heat grill to medium and grill the chops, turning occasionally, for 8-10 minutes or until cooked as desired.

Serve with the salad and a loaf of sourdough bread.   *Makes 4 servings*

Favorite recipe from **Meat and Livestock Australia**

Rosemary Steak

**4 boneless beef top loin (New York strip) steaks (about
     6 ounces each)**
2 tablespoons minced fresh rosemary
2 cloves garlic, minced
1 tablespoon extra-virgin olive oil
1 teaspoon grated lemon peel
1 teaspoon coarsely ground black pepper
½ teaspoon salt
     Fresh rosemary sprigs

Score steaks in diamond pattern on both sides. Combine minced
rosemary, garlic, oil, lemon peel, pepper and salt in small bowl; rub
mixture onto surface of meat. Cover and refrigerate at least 15 minutes.
Grill steaks over medium-hot KINGSFORD® Briquets about 4 minutes per
side until medium-rare or to desired doneness. Cut steaks diagonally into
½-inch-thick slices. Garnish with rosemary sprigs.   *Makes 4 servings*

Grilled Ham Steaks with Apricot Glaze

Prep Time: 15 minutes • **Cook Time:** 8 to 10 minutes

**1 pound boneless fully cooked ham, cut into
     4 (½-inch-thick) slices**
¼ cup apricot jam
2 teaspoons Dijon mustard
2 teaspoons cider vinegar

Prepare grill. Combine jam, mustard and vinegar in small bowl; blend
well. Grill ham slices over hot coals 8 to 10 minutes or until nicely
browned, brushing with apricot sauce occasionally and turning once.
Serve immediately.   *Makes 4 servings*

Favorite recipe from **National Pork Board**

Zesty Steak Fajitas

Prep Time: 5 minutes • **Cook Time:** 15 minutes
Marinate Time: 30 minutes

¾ **cup** *French's®* **Worcestershire Sauce, divided**
 1 **pound boneless top round, sirloin or flank steak**
 3 **tablespoons taco seasoning mix**
 2 **red or green bell peppers, cut into quarters**
 1 **to 2 large onions, cut into thick slices**
¾ **cup chili sauce**
 8 **(8-inch) flour or corn tortillas, heated**
   Sour cream and shredded cheese (optional)

1. Pour ½ cup Worcestershire over steak in deep dish. Cover and refrigerate 30 minutes or up to 3 hours. Drain meat and rub both sides with seasoning mix. Discard marinade.

2. Grill meat and vegetables over medium-hot coals 10 to 15 minutes until meat is medium rare (140°F) and vegetables are charred, but tender.

3. Thinly slice meat and vegetables. Place in large bowl. Add chili sauce and remaining ¼ cup Worcestershire. Toss to coat. Serve in tortillas and garnish with sour cream and cheese. *Makes 4 servings*

Guadalajara Beef and Salsa

1 bottle (12 ounces) Mexican dark beer*
¼ cup soy sauce
2 cloves garlic, minced
1 teaspoon ground cumin
1 teaspoon chili powder
1 teaspoon hot pepper sauce
4 boneless beef sirloin or top loin strip steaks (4 to 6 ounces each)
Salt and black pepper
Red, green and yellow bell peppers, cut lengthwise into quarters, seeded (optional)
Salsa (recipe follows)
Flour tortillas (optional)
Lime wedges

*You may substitute any beer for Mexican dark beer.

Combine beer, soy sauce, garlic, cumin, chili powder and hot pepper sauce in large shallow glass dish or large heavy plastic food storage bag. Add beef; cover dish or close bag. Marinate in refrigerator up to 12 hours, turning beef several times. Remove beef from marinade; discard marinade. Season with salt and black pepper.

Oil hot grid to help prevent sticking. Grill beef and bell peppers, if desired, on covered grill, over medium KINGSFORD® Briquets, 8 to 12 minutes, turning once. Beef should be of medium doneness (160°F) and peppers should be tender. Serve with salsa, tortillas, if desired, and lime wedges.

Makes 4 servings

Salsa

2 cups coarsely chopped seeded tomatoes
2 green onions with tops, sliced
1 clove garlic, minced
1 to 2 teaspoons minced seeded jalapeño or serrano chili pepper,* fresh or canned
1 tablespoon olive or vegetable oil
2 to 3 teaspoons lime juice

8 to 10 sprigs fresh cilantro, minced (optional)
½ teaspoon salt or to taste
½ teaspoon sugar or to taste
¼ teaspoon black pepper

*Jalapeño peppers can sting and irritate the skin; wear rubber gloves when handling and do not touch your eyes.

Combine tomatoes, green onions, garlic, chili pepper, oil and lime juice in medium bowl. Stir in cilantro, if desired. Season with salt, sugar and black pepper. Adjust seasonings to taste, adding lime juice or chili pepper, if desired. *Makes about 2 cups*

Steak Provençal

4 beef ribeye, sirloin or tenderloin steaks (about 11 ounces each)
5 tablespoons I CAN'T BELIEVE IT'S NOT BUTTER!® Spread
2 large cloves garlic, finely chopped
1½ cups chopped tomatoes (about 2 medium)
1 to 2 tablespoons rinsed and chopped large capers
¼ teaspoon salt
¼ teaspoon ground black pepper
2 tablespoons chopped fresh parsley

Grill or broil steaks to desired doneness.

Meanwhile, in 10-inch skillet, melt I Can't Believe It's Not Butter!® Spread and cook garlic over medium heat, stirring occasionally, 30 seconds. Add tomatoes, capers, salt and pepper. Cook, stirring occasionally, 3 minutes or until tomatoes are cooked and mixture is saucy. Stir in parsley. Serve over hot steaks. *Makes 4 servings*

Drunken T-Bone Steak

Prep Time: 5 minutes • **Cook Time:** 15 minutes • **Marinate Time:** 1 hour

2 T-bone steaks, cut 1-inch thick (about 3 pounds)
1 cup *French's*® Worcestershire Sauce
½ cup *Cattlemen's*® Authentic Smoke House Barbecue Sauce
3 tablespoons bourbon
2 tablespoons butter
2 tablespoons *French's*® Worcestershire Sauce
4 teaspoons garlic and pepper steak seasoning

1. Place steaks into resealable plastic food storage bag. Pour 1 cup Worcestershire over steaks. Marinate in refrigerator 1 to 3 hours.

2. Meanwhile, prepare sauce. Combine barbecue sauce, bourbon, butter and 2 tablespoons Worcestershire in saucepan. Heat to boiling. Simmer 3 minutes; reserve.

3. Drain steaks. Rub steak seasoning into meat, coating both sides. Cook steaks over high direct heat, about 7 minutes per side for medium-rare or to desired doneness. Let steaks rest 10 minutes before slicing. Serve with sauce on the side.   *Makes 4 servings*

Grilled Pork Tenderloin Medallions

> **1 tablespoon garlic salt**
> **1 tablespoon dried basil**
> **1 tablespoon dried thyme**
> **1½ teaspoons cracked black pepper**
> **1½ teaspoons dried rosemary**
> **1 teaspoon paprika**
> **Olive oil cooking spray**
> **12 pork tenderloin medallions (about 1 pound)**

1. For rub, combine garlic salt, basil, thyme, pepper, rosemary and paprika in small jar or resealable food storage bag.

2. Spray cold grid of grill with cooking spray. Prepare grill for direct grilling. Sprinkle 2 tablespoons rub evenly over both sides of pork, pressing lightly. Spray pork with cooking spray.

3. Place pork on grid over medium-hot coals. Grill, uncovered, 4 to 5 minutes per side or until pork is barely pink in center.

Makes 4 servings

Serving Suggestion: Serve with steamed red potatoes and yellow bell pepper strips, if desired.

Lamb Chops with Cranberry-Orange Salsa

1 medium orange, sectioned and chopped *or* ½ cup canned mandarin oranges, chopped
¼ cup finely chopped onion
¼ cup chopped green chilies, drained
¼ cup dried cranberries
¼ cup orange marmalade
1 tablespoon finely chopped cilantro
1 tablespoon vinegar
2 tablespoons orange juice
1 teaspoon Worcestershire sauce
8 American lamb loin chops, 1 inch thick (about 2 pounds)

For salsa, combine orange, onion, chilies, cranberries, marmalade, cilantro and vinegar. Cover; chill several hours. Combine orange juice and Worcestershire. Brush lamb with juice mixture. Grill over medium coals or broil 4 inches from heat source for 5 minutes. Turn and grill or broil 4 to 6 minutes longer or to medium doneness. Serve with salsa.

Makes 4 servings

Favorite recipe from **American Lamb Council**

Mojo Pork with Orange-Apple Salsa

Prep Time: 15 minutes • **Cook Time:** 35 minutes
Marinate Time: 1 hour

2 tablespoons olive oil
1 tablespoon minced garlic
½ cup Frank's® RedHot® Chile 'n Lime™ Hot Sauce
½ cup orange juice
2 tablespoons grated orange zest
¼ cup minced cilantro
2 tablespoons chili powder
1 teaspoon oregano leaves
2 boneless pork tenderloins (2 pounds)
½ cup sour cream
  Orange-Apple Salsa (recipe follows)

1. Sauté garlic in hot oil; cool. Slowly stir in *Chile 'n Lime™* Hot Sauce, orange juice, zest, cilantro, chili powder and oregano. Reserve ¼ cup marinade.

2. Place pork into resealable plastic food storage bags. Pour remaining marinade over pork. Seal bag; marinate in refrigerator 1 to 3 hours. Combine remaining marinade with sour cream; set aside in refrigerator.

3. Grill pork over medium-high direct heat for 30 minutes until no longer pink in center (155°F). Slice pork and drizzle with spicy sour cream. Serve with Orange-Apple Salsa. *Makes 6 to 8 servings*

Orange-Apple Salsa

3 navel oranges, peeled, sectioned and cut into small pieces
2 large apples, cored and cut into small dice
2 tablespoons chopped red onion
2 tablespoons chopped cilantro
2 tablespoons Frank's® RedHot® Chile 'n Lime™ Hot Sauce

Combine ingredients in bowl; chill until ready to serve.
Makes about 3 cups

Peppered Steak with Dijon Sauce

Prep Time: 10 minutes • **Cook Time:** 15 minutes

4 boneless beef top loin (New York strip) steaks, cut 1 inch thick (about 1½ pounds)
1 tablespoon *French's*® Worcestershire Sauce
Crushed black pepper
⅓ cup mayonnaise
⅓ cup *French's*® Honey Dijon Mustard
3 tablespoons dry red wine
2 tablespoons minced red or green onion
2 tablespoons minced fresh parsley
1 clove garlic, minced

1. Prepare grill for direct cooking. Brush steaks with Worcestershire and sprinkle with pepper to taste; set aside. To prepare Dijon sauce, combine mayonnaise, mustard, wine, onion, parsley and garlic in medium bowl.

2. Place steaks on grid. Grill steaks over high heat 15 minutes for medium rare (140°F) or to desired doneness, turning often. Serve with Dijon sauce. Garnish with peppercorns as desired.   *Makes 4 servings*

Tip: Dijon sauce is also great served with grilled salmon and swordfish. To serve with fish, substitute white wine for red wine and minced dill for fresh parsley.

Grilled Honey Garlic Pork Chops

¼ **cup lemon juice**
¼ **cup honey**
2 **tablespoons soy sauce**
1 **tablespoon dry sherry**
2 **cloves garlic, minced**
4 **boneless center-cut lean pork chops (about ¼ pound each)**

Combine all ingredients except pork chops in small bowl. Place pork in shallow baking dish; pour marinade over pork. Cover and refrigerate 4 hours or overnight. Remove pork from marinade. Heat remaining marinade in small saucepan over medium heat to a simmer. Grill pork over medium-hot coals 12 to 15 minutes, turning once during cooking and basting frequently with marinade, until meat thermometer registers 155° to 160°F. Do not baste during last 5 minutes of grilling.

Makes 4 servings

Favorite recipe from **National Honey Board**

**Spiced Turkey
with Fruit Salsa (p. 60)**

**Nancy's Grilled
Turkey Meatballs (p. 70)**

Grilled Chicken Adobo (p. 64)   Glazed Cornish Hens (p. 78)

Quick Clucks

Spicy Barbecued Chicken

1 tablespoon paprika or smoked paprika
1 teaspoon dried thyme
½ teaspoon salt
½ teaspoon dried sage
¼ teaspoon black pepper
¼ teaspoon ground red pepper
1 chicken, quartered (3½ to 4 pounds)
¾ cup ketchup
½ cup packed light brown sugar
2 tablespoons soy sauce
2 tablespoons Worcestershire sauce
1 large clove garlic, minced

1. Combine paprika, thyme, salt, sage and black and red peppers. Rub mixture over all sides of chicken. Transfer chicken to food storage bag; refrigerate up to 24 hours.

2. For barbecue sauce, combine remaining ingredients in medium bowl; mix well.

3. Prepare grill for direct cooking. Place chicken on grid, meaty sides up, over medium to medium-low coals. Cover grill and cook 30 to 40 minutes, turning once, or until chicken is cooked through (170°F for breast meat; 180°F for dark meat).

4. Turn chicken meaty sides up. Reserve half of barbecue sauce for serving; brush half over chicken. Grill, covered, about 5 minutes on each side to glaze. Serve with reserved sauce.

Makes 4 servings

Grilled Rosemary Chicken

Prep and Cook Time: 30 minutes

2 tablespoons minced fresh rosemary
2 tablespoons lemon juice
2 tablespoons olive oil
2 cloves garlic, minced
¼ teaspoon salt
4 boneless skinless chicken breasts (about 1 pound)

1. Spray cold grid of grill with nonstick cooking spray. Prepare grill for direct cooking.

2. Whisk together rosemary, lemon juice, oil, garlic and salt in small bowl. Pour into shallow glass dish. Add chicken, turning to coat both sides with lemon juice mixture. Cover; marinate in refrigerator 15 minutes, turning chicken once. Remove chicken; discard marinade.

3. Grill chicken over medium-hot coals 5 to 6 minutes per side or until chicken is no longer pink in center. Serve with grilled or steamed fresh vegetables; if desired. *Makes 4 servings*

Cook's Note: For added flavor, moisten a few sprigs of fresh rosemary and toss on the hot coals just before grilling.

Tip: To store fresh rosemary, wrap sprigs in a barely damp paper towel and place in a sealed plastic bag. It can be kept in the refrigerator for up to five days.

Spiced Turkey with Fruit Salsa

6 ounces turkey breast tenderloin
2 teaspoons lime juice
1 teaspoon mesquite seasoning blend or ground cumin
½ cup frozen pitted sweet cherries, thawed and cut into halves*
¼ cup chunky salsa

Drained canned sweet cherries can be substituted for frozen cherries.

1. Prepare grill for direct grilling. Brush both sides of turkey with lime juice. Sprinkle with mesquite seasoning.

2. Grill turkey over medium heat 15 to 20 minutes or until turkey is no longer pink in center and juices run clear, turning once.

3. Meanwhile, stir together cherries and salsa.

4. Thinly slice turkey. To serve, spoon salsa mixture over turkey.

Makes 2 servings

Herb Garlic Grilled Chicken

¼ cup chopped fresh parsley
1½ tablespoons minced garlic
4 teaspoons grated lemon peel
1 tablespoon chopped fresh mint
1 chicken (2½ to 3 pounds), quartered

Combine parsley, garlic, lemon peel and mint. Loosen skin from breast and thigh portions of chicken quarters by running fingers between skin and meat. Rub some of seasoning mixture evenly over meat under skin, replace skin and rub remaining seasonings over outside of chicken to cover evenly. Arrange medium-hot KINGSFORD® Briquets on one side of covered grill. Place chicken on grid opposite coals. Cover grill and cook chicken 45 to 55 minutes, turning once or twice. Chicken is done when juices run clear (180°F for dark meat). *Makes 4 servings*

Grilled Lemon Chicken Dijon

⅓ cup HOLLAND HOUSE® White with Lemon Cooking Wine
⅓ cup olive oil
2 tablespoons Dijon mustard
1 teaspoon dried thyme leaves
2 whole chicken breasts, skinned, boned and halved

In shallow baking dish combine cooking wine, oil, mustard and thyme. Add chicken and turn to coat. Cover; marinate in refrigerator for 1 to 2 hours.

Prepare grill for direct cooking. Drain chicken, reserving marinade. Grill chicken over medium coals 12 to 16 minutes or until cooked through, turning once and basting with marinade.*   *Makes 4 servings*

Do not baste during last 5 minutes of grilling.

Chicken Teriyaki

8 large chicken drumsticks (about 2 pounds)
⅓ cup teriyaki sauce
2 tablespoons brandy or apple juice
1 green onion, minced
1 tablespoon vegetable oil
1 teaspoon ground ginger
½ teaspoon sugar
¼ teaspoon garlic powder
Prepared sweet and sour sauce (optional)

1. Remove skin from drumsticks, if desired, by pulling skin toward end of leg using paper towel; discard skin.

2. Place chicken in large resealable food storage bag. Combine teriyaki sauce, brandy, onion, oil, ginger, sugar and garlic powder in small bowl; pour over chicken. Close bag securely, turning to coat. Marinate in refrigerator at least 1 hour or overnight, turning occasionally.

continued on page 64

Grilled Lemon Chicken Dijon, continued

3. Prepare grill for indirect cooking.

4. Drain chicken; reserve marinade. Place chicken on grid directly over drip pan. Grill, covered, over medium-high heat 60 minutes or until chicken is cooked through (170°F), turning and brushing with reserved marinade every 20 minutes. *Do not brush with marinade during last 5 minutes of grilling.* Discard remaining marinade. Serve with sweet and sour sauce, if desired.   *Makes 4 servings*

Grilled Chicken Adobo

> **½ cup chopped onion**
> **⅓ cup lime juice**
> **6 cloves garlic, coarsely chopped**
> **1 teaspoon dried oregano**
> **1 teaspoon ground cumin**
> **½ teaspoon dried thyme**
> **¼ teaspoon ground red pepper**
> **6 boneless skinless chicken breasts (about 1½ pounds)**
> **3 tablespoons chopped fresh cilantro**

1. Combine onion, lime juice and garlic in food processor. Process until onion is finely minced. Transfer to large resealable food storage bag. Add oregano, cumin, thyme and red pepper; knead bag until blended. Place chicken in bag; press out air and seal. Turn to coat chicken with marinade. Refrigerate 30 minutes or up to 4 hours.

2. Spray grid with nonstick cooking spray. Prepare grill for direct cooking. Remove chicken from marinade; discard marinade. Place chicken on grid 3 to 4 inches from medium-hot coals. Grill 5 to 7 minutes on each side or until chicken is no longer pink in center. Transfer to clean serving platter and sprinkle with cilantro.   *Makes 6 servings*

Thai Grilled Chicken

Prep and Cook Time: 25 minutes

4 boneless skinless chicken breasts (about 1¼ pounds)
¼ cup soy sauce
2 teaspoons minced garlic
½ teaspoon red pepper flakes
2 tablespoons honey
1 tablespoon fresh lime juice

1. Prepare grill for direct cooking. Place chicken in shallow baking dish. Combine soy sauce, garlic and pepper flakes in measuring cup. Pour over chicken, turning to coat. Let stand 10 minutes.

2. Meanwhile, combine honey and lime juice in small bowl until blended; set aside.

3. Place chicken on grid over medium coals; brush with marinade. Discard remaining marinade. Grill, covered, 5 minutes. Brush both sides of chicken with honey mixture. Grill 5 minutes more or until chicken is no longer pink in center. *Makes 4 servings*

Serving Suggestion: Serve with steamed white rice, Oriental vegetables and fresh fruit salad.

Grilled Garlic Chicken

1 envelope LIPTON® RECIPE SECRETS® Savory Herb with Garlic Soup Mix
3 tablespoons BERTOLLI® Olive Oil
4 boneless, skinless chicken breast halves (about 1¼ pounds)

1. In medium bowl, combine soup mix with oil.

2. Add chicken; toss to coat.

3. Grill or broil until chicken is thoroughly cooked. *Makes 4 servings*

Jamaican Rum Chicken

½ cup dark rum
2 tablespoons lime juice or lemon juice
2 tablespoons soy sauce
2 tablespoons brown sugar
4 large cloves garlic, minced
1 to 2 jalapeño peppers,* seeded and minced
1 tablespoon minced fresh ginger
1 teaspoon dried thyme
½ teaspoon black pepper
6 boneless skinless chicken breasts (about 1½ pounds)

*Jalapeño peppers can sting and irritate the skin, so wear rubber gloves when handling peppers and do not touch your eyes.

1. To prepare marinade, combine rum, lime juice, soy sauce, sugar, garlic, peppers, ginger, thyme and black pepper in 2-quart glass measuring cup.

2. Place chicken in large resealable food storage bag; pour marinade over chicken. Press air out of bag and seal tightly. Turn bag over to completely coat chicken with marinade. Refrigerate 4 hours or overnight, turning bag once or twice.

3. Prepare grill for direct cooking. Drain chicken; reserve marinade. Place chicken on grid. Grill chicken on uncovered grill over medium-hot coals 6 minutes per side or until chicken is no longer pink in center.

4. Meanwhile, bring remaining marinade to a boil in small saucepan over medium-high heat. Boil 5 minutes or until marinade is reduced by about half.

5. To serve, drizzle marinade over chicken. Garnish as desired.

Makes 6 servings

Lime-Mustard Marinated Chicken

2 boneless skinless chicken breasts
¼ cup fresh lime juice
3 tablespoons honey mustard, divided
2 teaspoons olive oil
¼ teaspoon ground cumin
⅛ teaspoon garlic powder
⅛ teaspoon ground red pepper
¾ cup plus 2 tablespoons reduced-sodium chicken broth, divided
¼ cup uncooked rice
1 cup broccoli florets
1 medium carrot, cut into matchstick-size pieces

1. Place chicken in resealable food storage bag. Whisk together lime juice, 2 tablespoons mustard, olive oil, cumin, garlic powder and red pepper. Pour over chicken. Seal bag. Marinate in refrigerator 2 hours.

2. Combine ¾ cup chicken broth, rice and remaining 1 tablespoon mustard in small saucepan. Bring to a boil. Reduce heat and simmer, covered, 12 minutes or until rice is almost tender. Stir in broccoli, carrots and remaining 2 tablespoons chicken broth. Cook, covered, 2 to 3 minutes more or until vegetables are crisp-tender and rice is tender.

3. Meanwhile, drain chicken, discard marinade. Prepare grill for direct grilling. Grill chicken over medium coals 10 to 13 minutes or until no longer pink in center. Serve chicken with rice mixture.

Makes 2 servings

Nancy's Grilled Turkey Meatballs

Prep Time: 15 minutes • **Cook Time:** 10 minutes

1 pound lean ground turkey breast
½ cup oatmeal
¼ cup fresh whole wheat bread crumbs
1 egg white
3 tablespoons fat-free or reduced-fat Parmesan cheese
2 tablespoons *French's*® Honey Dijon Mustard
¼ teaspoon crushed garlic
¼ teaspoon ground black pepper
1 cup pineapple chunks or wedges
1 small red bell pepper, cut into squares

1. Combine turkey, oatmeal, bread crumbs, egg white, cheese, mustard, garlic and black pepper in large bowl. Mix well and form into 24 meatballs.

2. Place 4 meatballs on each skewer, alternating with pineapple and bell pepper.

3. Cook meatballs 10 minutes on well greased grill over medium heat until no longer pink inside (165°F), turning often. Serve with additional **French's**® Honey Dijon Mustard on the side for dipping.

Makes 6 servings

Tip: Combine 1/3 cup each French's® Honey Dijon Mustard, honey and Frank's® RedHot® Cayenne Pepper Sauce. Use for dipping grilled wings, ribs and chicken.

Garlic & Lemon Herb Marinated Chicken

Prep Time: 10 minutes • **Cook Time:** 45 minutes
Marinate Time: 1 hour

3 to 4 pounds bone-in chicken pieces, skinned if desired
⅓ cup *French's*® Honey Dijon Mustard
⅓ cup lemon juice
⅓ cup olive oil
3 cloves garlic, minced
1 tablespoon grated lemon zest
1 tablespoon minced fresh thyme or rosemary
1 teaspoon coarse salt
½ teaspoon coarse black pepper

1. Place chicken into resealable plastic food storage bag. Combine remaining ingredients. Pour over chicken. Marinate in refrigerator 1 to 3 hours.

2. Remove chicken from marinade. Grill chicken over medium direct heat for 35 to 45 minutes until juices run clear near bone (180°F for dark meat). Serve with additional mustard on the side.   *Makes 4 servings*

Tip: This marinade is great on whole chicken or pork chops.

Classic Grilled Chicken

1 whole frying chicken* (3½ pounds), quartered
¼ cup lemon juice
¼ cup olive oil
2 tablespoons soy sauce
2 large cloves garlic, minced
½ teaspoon sugar
½ teaspoon ground cumin
¼ teaspoon black pepper

*Substitute 3½ pounds chicken parts for whole chicken, if desired. Grill legs and thighs about 35 minutes and breast halves about 25 minutes or until chicken is cooked through (180°F for dark meat), turning once.

Rinse chicken under cold running water; pat dry with paper towels. Arrange chicken in 13×9×2-inch glass baking dish. Combine remaining ingredients in small bowl; pour half of mixture over chicken. Cover and refrigerate chicken at least 1 hour or overnight. Cover and reserve remaining mixture in refrigerator to use for basting. Remove chicken from marinade; discard marinade. Arrange medium KINGSFORD® Briquets on each side of large rectangular metal or foil drip pan. Pour hot tap water into drip pan until half full. Place chicken on grid directly above drip pan. Grill chicken, skin side down, on covered grill 25 minutes. Baste with reserved mixture. Turn chicken; cook 20 to 25 minutes or until juices run clear and chicken is cooked through (180°F for dark meat).

Makes 6 servings

Grilled Chicken with Spicy Black Beans & Rice

2 boneless skinless chicken breasts (about ½ pound)
½ teaspoon Caribbean jerk seasoning
½ teaspoon olive oil
¼ cup finely diced green bell pepper
2 teaspoons chipotle chili powder
¾ cup hot cooked rice
½ cup rinsed and drained canned black beans
2 tablespoons diced pimiento
1 tablespoon chopped pimiento-stuffed green olives
1 tablespoon chopped onion
1 tablespoon chopped fresh cilantro (optional)
Lime wedges for garnish (optional)

1. Spray cold grid of grill with nonstick cooking spray. Prepare grill for direct grilling. Rub chicken with jerk seasoning. Grill over medium-hot coals 8 to 10 minutes or until no longer pink in center.

2. Meanwhile, heat oil in medium saucepan or skillet over medium heat. Add bell pepper and chili powder; cook and stir until peppers are soft.

3. Add rice, beans, pimiento and olives to saucepan. Cook about 3 minutes or until hot.

4. Serve bean mixture with chicken. Top bean mixture with onion and cilantro, if desired. Garnish with lime wedges. *Makes 2 servings*

Glazed Cornish Hens

2 fresh or thawed frozen Cornish game hens (1½ pounds each)
3 tablespoons fresh lemon juice
1 clove garlic, minced
¼ cup orange marmalade
1 tablespoon coarse-grain or country-style mustard
2 teaspoons grated fresh ginger

1. Remove giblets from cavities of hens; reserve for another use. Split hens in half on cutting board with sharp knife or poultry shears, cutting through breast bones and backbones. Rinse hens with cold water; pat dry with paper towels. Place hen halves in large resealable food storage bag.

2. Combine juice and garlic in small bowl; pour over hens in bag. Seal bag tightly, turning to coat. Marinate in refrigerator 30 minutes.

3. Meanwhile, prepare grill for direct grilling over medium-hot heat.

4. Drain hens; discard marinade. Place hens, skin sides up, on grid. Grill hens on covered grill over medium-hot coals 20 minutes.

5. Meanwhile, combine marmalade, mustard and ginger in small bowl. Brush half of marmalade mixture evenly over hens. Grill, covered, 10 minutes. Brush with remaining mixture. Grill, covered, 5 to 10 minutes more until fork can be inserted into hens with ease and juices run clear (170°F for breast meat). Serve immediately.   *Makes 4 servings*

Grilled Sherry Pork Chop (p. 102)   **Backyard Barbecue Burger (p. 96)**

Grilled Mesquite Vegetables
(p. 82)

Peachy Smothered
Pork Chop (p. 88)

Grill Greats

Grilled Mesquite Vegetables

Preparation Time: 10 minutes • **Cooking Time:** 10 minutes

2 to 3 tablespoons MRS. DASH® Mesquite Grilling Blend
2 tablespoons olive oil, divided
1 eggplant, trimmed and cut into ½-inch slices
1 zucchini, quartered lengthwise
1 red onion, peeled and halved
2 red bell peppers, cut into large slices
2 green bell peppers, cut into large slices
1 tablespoon balsamic vinegar

Preheat barbecue grill to medium. In large bowl, combine Mrs. Dash®
Mesquite Grilling Blend and 1 tablespoon olive oil. Add vegetables and
toss until well coated with olive oil mixture. Place vegetables on grill.
Cover and cook, turning vegetables once during cooking, until vegetables
are tender and develop grill marks, about 3 to 4 minutes on each side.
Remove vegetables from grill as soon as they are cooked. Coarsely chop
vegetables into ½-inch pieces. Mix remaining olive oil and balsamic
vinegar in large bowl. Add cut vegetables and toss to coat. Serve at room
temperature.   *Makes 6 servings*

Note: Grilling vegetables dehydrates them slightly and intensifies flavors
while Mrs. Dash Mesquite adds a third dimension of flavor. This dish
makes a colorful accompaniment to any grilled meat.

Marinated Italian Sausage and Peppers

½ **cup olive oil**
¼ **cup red wine vinegar**
2 **tablespoons chopped fresh parsley**
1 **tablespoon dried oregano**
2 **cloves garlic, crushed**
1 **teaspoon salt**
1 **teaspoon black pepper**
4 **hot or sweet Italian sausages**
1 **large onion, cut into rings**
1 **large bell pepper, cut into quarters**
  Horseradish-Mustard Spread (recipe follows)

1. Combine oil, vinegar, parsley, oregano, garlic, salt and black pepper in small bowl. Place sausages, onion and bell pepper in large resealable food storage bag; pour oil mixture into bag. Close bag securely, turning to coat. Marinate in refrigerator 1 to 2 hours.

2. Prepare Horseradish-Mustard Spread; set aside. Prepare grill for direct cooking. Drain sausages, onion and bell pepper; discard marinade.

3. Grill sausages, covered, 4 to 5 minutes. Turn sausages and place onion and bell pepper on grid. Grill, covered, 5 minutes or until vegetables are crisp-tender, turning vegetables halfway through grilling time. Serve sausages, onions and bell peppers with Horseradish-Mustard Spread.

Makes 4 servings

Horseradish-Mustard Spread

3 tablespoons mayonnaise
1 tablespoon chopped fresh parsley
1 tablespoon prepared horseradish
1 tablespoon Dijon mustard
2 teaspoons garlic powder
1 teaspoon black pepper

Combine all ingredients in small bowl; mix well. *Makes about ½ cup*

Peppercorn
Steaks

2 tablespoons olive oil
1 to 2 teaspoons cracked pink or black peppercorns or freshly ground pepper
1 teaspoon minced garlic
1 teaspoon dried herbs, such as rosemary or parsley
4 boneless beef top loin (strip) or ribeye steaks (6 ounces each)
¼ teaspoon salt

1. Combine oil, peppercorns, garlic and herbs in small bowl. Rub mixture on both sides of each steak. Cover and refrigerate. Prepare grill for direct cooking.

2. Place steaks on grid over medium heat. Grill, uncovered, 10 to 12 minutes for medium-rare to medium (160°F) or to desired doneness, turning once. Season with salt after cooking. *Makes 4 servings*

Beef with Dry Spice Rub

3 tablespoons firmly packed brown sugar
1 tablespoon yellow mustard seeds
1 tablespoon whole coriander seeds
1 tablespoon black peppercorns
4 cloves garlic
1½ to 2 pounds beef top round (London Broil) steak, about 1½ inches thick
Vegetable or olive oil
Salt

Place sugar, mustard seeds, coriander seeds, peppercorns and garlic in blender or food processor; process until seeds and garlic are crushed. Rub beef with oil; pat on spice mixture. Season generously with salt.

Lightly oil hot grid to prevent sticking. Grill beef, on covered grill, over medium-low KINGSFORD® Briquets 16 to 20 minutes for medium rare (140°F) or until desired doneness, turning once. Let stand 5 minutes before cutting across the grain into thin diagonal slices. *Makes 6 servings*

Peachy Smothered Pork Chops

Prep Time: 5 minutes • **Cook Time:** 25 minutes

1 tablespoon vegetable oil
1 small onion, finely minced
1 (12 ounce) jar peach preserves
⅔ cup *French's*® Honey Mustard
2 teaspoons grated peeled gingerroot
¼ teaspoon ground nutmeg
6 boneless pork chops, cut 1-inch thick

1. Heat oil in small saucepan; sauté onion until tender. Stir in peach preserves, mustard, ginger and nutmeg. Heat to boiling; simmer 5 minutes until flavors are blended. Transfer ¾ cup sauce to bowl for basting. Reserve remaining sauce; keep warm.

2. Grill or broil chops over medium direct heat 20 minutes until barely pink in center, turning and basting often with sauce.

3. Serve chops with reserved sauce mixture. *Makes 6 servings*

Alternate Method: For alternate skillet method, brown chops in skillet. Pour peach mixture over chops and simmer until no longer pink in center.

Rustic Texas-Que Pizza

Prep Time: 15 minutes • **Cook Time:** 10 minutes

2 cups shredded, cooked chicken (about 1 pound uncooked)
¼ cup *Frank's® RedHot® Chile 'n Lime™* Hot Sauce or *Frank's® RedHot®* Buffalo Wing Sauce
1 pound prepared pizza or bread dough (thawed, if frozen)
Vegetable Oil Cooking Spray
1 cup *Cattlemen's®* Award Winning Classic Barbecue Sauce
2 ripe plum tomatoes, ¼-inch dice
½ cup finely diced red onion
½ cup sliced black olives (2.25 ounce can)
2 cups shredded taco blend cheese
Cilantro or green onions, minced (optional)

1. Toss chicken with *Chile 'n Lime™* Hot Sauce, set aside. Divide dough in half. Gently stretch or roll each piece of dough into a 13×9-inch rectangle on floured surface. Coat one side with cooking spray.

2. Cook dough, coated side down, on greased grill over medium-high heat for 5 minutes until browned and crisp on bottom. Using tongs, turn dough over. Spread each pizza crust with barbecue sauce and top with chicken mixture, tomatoes, onion, olives and cheese, dividing evenly.

3. Grill pizzas about 5 minutes longer until bottom is browned, crispy and cheese melts. Garnish with minced cilantro or green onions, if desired.

Makes 8 servings

Variation: Top pizza with different shredded cheeses, such as Cheddar or Jack, or with other vegetables, such as whole kernel corn, jalapeño or bell peppers.

Tip: For easier handling, allow pizza dough to rest 30 minutes in an oiled, covered bowl at room temperature.

Maple Francheezies

Mustard Spread (recipe follows)
¼ cup maple syrup
2 teaspoons garlic powder
1 teaspoon black pepper
½ teaspoon ground nutmeg
4 slices bacon
4 jumbo hot dogs
4 hot dog buns, split
½ cup (2 ounces) shredded Cheddar cheese

1. Prepare Mustard Spread; set aside.

2. Prepare grill for direct cooking.

3. Combine maple syrup, garlic powder, pepper and nutmeg in small bowl. Brush syrup mixture onto bacon slices. Wrap 1 slice bacon around each hot dog.

4. Brush hot dogs with remaining syrup mixture. Place hot dogs on grid. Grill, covered, over medium-high heat 8 minutes or until bacon is crisp and hot dogs are heated through, turning halfway through grilling time. Place hot dogs in buns, top with Mustard Spread and cheese.

Makes 4 servings

Mustard Spread

½ cup prepared yellow mustard
1 tablespoon finely chopped onion
1 tablespoon diced tomato
1 tablespoon chopped fresh parsley
1 teaspoon garlic powder
½ teaspoon black pepper

Combine all ingredients in small bowl; mix well.

Makes about ¾ cup

Southern Barbecue Sandwich

Prep Time: 15 minutes • **Marinate Time:** 20 minutes
Cook Time: 25 minutes

1 pound boneless beef top sirloin or flank steak*
¾ cup *French's*® Worcestershire Sauce, divided
½ cup ketchup
½ cup light molasses
¼ cup *French's*® Classic Yellow® Mustard
2 tablespoons *Frank's*® RedHot® Original Cayenne Pepper Sauce
½ teaspoon hickory salt
4 sandwich buns, split

*You can also substitute 1 pound pork tenderloin for the steak. Cook pork until meat is juicy and barely pink in center or substitute leftover sliced steak for the grilled steak. Stir into sauce and heat through.

1. Place steak in large resealable plastic food storage bag. Pour ½ cup Worcestershire over steak. Seal bag and marinate meat in refrigerator 20 minutes.

2. To prepare barbecue sauce, combine ketchup, molasses, remaining ¼ cup Worcestershire, mustard, **Frank's RedHot** Sauce and hickory salt in medium saucepan. Bring to a boil over high heat. Reduce heat to low. Cook 5 minutes until slightly thickened, stirring occasionally. Set aside.

3. Place steak on grid, discarding marinade. Grill over hot coals 15 minutes, turning once. Remove steak from grid; let stand 5 minutes. Cut steak diagonally into thin slices. Stir meat into barbecue sauce. Cook until heated through, stirring often. Serve steak and sauce in sandwich buns. Garnish as desired.   *Makes 4 servings*

Shrimp on the Barbie

Prep Time: 10 minutes • **Cook Time:** 15 minutes

1 pound large raw shrimp, shelled and deveined
1 *each* red and yellow bell peppers, seeded and cut into 1-inch chunks
4 slices lime (optional)
½ cup prepared smoky-flavor barbecue sauce
2 tablespoons *French's*® Worcestershire Sauce
2 tablespoons *Frank's*® *RedHot*® Original Cayenne Pepper Sauce
1 clove garlic, minced

Thread shrimp, peppers and lime, if desired, alternately onto metal skewers. Combine barbecue sauce, Worcestershire, **Frank's RedHot** Sauce and garlic in small bowl; mix well. Brush on skewers.

Place skewers on grid, reserving remaining sauce mixture. Grill over hot coals 15 minutes or until shrimp turn pink, turning and basting often with sauce mixture. (Do not baste during last 5 minutes of cooking.) Serve warm.   *Makes 4 servings*

Backyard Barbecue Burgers

1½ pounds ground beef
⅓ cup barbecue sauce, divided
1 to 2 tomatoes, cut into slices
1 onion, cut into thick slices
1 to 2 tablespoons olive oil
6 kaiser rolls, split
6 leaves green or red leaf lettuce

1. Prepare grill for direct grilling. Combine ground beef and 2 tablespoons barbecue sauce in large bowl. Shape into six 1-inch-thick patties.

2. Place patties on grid over medium heat. Grill, covered, 8 to 10 minutes (or, uncovered, 13 to 15 minutes) for medium doneness or until 160°F in centers of patties, turning and brushing often with remaining barbecue sauce.

3. Meanwhile, brush tomato and onion slices* with oil. Place on grid. Grill tomato slices 2 to 3 minutes and onion slices about 10 minutes.

4. Just before serving, place rolls, cut side down, on grid; grill until lightly toasted. Serve patties on rolls with tomatoes, onions and lettuce.

Makes 6 servings

*Onion slices may be cooked in 2 tablespoons oil in large skillet over medium heat 10 minutes until tender and slightly brown.

Hot, Spicy, Tangy, Sticky Chicken

1 chicken (3½ to 4 pounds), cut up
1 cup cider vinegar
1 tablespoon Worcestershire sauce
1 tablespoon chili powder
1 teaspoon salt
1 teaspoon black pepper
1 teaspoon hot pepper sauce
¾ cup KC MASTERPIECE™ Original Barbecue Sauce

Place chicken in shallow glass dish or large heavy plastic bag. Combine vinegar, Worcestershire sauce, chili powder, salt, black pepper and hot pepper sauce in small bowl; pour over chicken pieces. Cover dish or seal bag. Marinate in refrigerator at least 4 hours, turning several times.

Oil hot grid to prevent sticking. Place dark meat pieces on grill 10 minutes before white meat pieces (dark meat takes longer to cook). Grill chicken on a covered grill, over medium KINGSFORD® Briquets, 30 to 45 minutes, turning once or twice. Turn and baste with KC MASTERPIECE™ Original Barbecue Sauce the last 10 minutes of cooking. Remove chicken from grill; baste with barbecue sauce. Chicken is done when meat is no longer pink near bone (170°F for breast meat; 180°F for dark meat).

Makes 4 servings

Brats 'n' Beer

1 can or bottle (12 ounces) beer (not dark)
4 bratwurst (about 1 pound)
1 sweet or Spanish onion, thinly sliced and separated into rings
1 tablespoon olive oil
¼ teaspoon salt
¼ teaspoon black pepper
4 hot dog rolls

1. Prepare coals for direct grilling.

2. Pour beer into heavy medium saucepan with ovenproof handle. (If not ovenproof, wrap heavy-duty foil around handle.) Place saucepan on grill.

3. Pierce bratwurst with knife; add to beer. Simmer, uncovered, over medium coals 15 minutes, turning once during cooking.

4. Place onion rings on heavy-duty foil. Drizzle with oil; sprinkle with salt and pepper. Fold sides of foil over rings to enclose. Place packets on grill. Grill, uncovered, 10 to 15 minutes or until onion rings are tender.

5. Transfer bratwurst to grill. Remove saucepan from grill; discard beer. Grill bratwurst 10 minutes or until browned and cooked through (160°F), turning once during grilling.

6. Place bratwurst in rolls. Top with onions. Garnish as desired.

Makes 4 servings

Grilled Sherry Pork Chops

¼ cup HOLLAND HOUSE® Sherry Cooking Wine
¼ cup GRANDMA'S® Molasses
2 tablespoons soy sauce
4 pork chops (1 inch thick)

In plastic bowl, combine sherry, molasses and soy sauce; pour over pork chops. Cover; refrigerate 30 minutes. Prepare grill. Drain pork chops; reserve marinade. Grill pork chops over medium-high heat 20 to 30 minutes or until pork is no longer pink in center (155°F), turning once and brushing frequently with reserved marinade.* Discard any remaining marinade.   *Makes 4 servings*

Do not baste during last 5 minutes of grilling.

The Definitive Steak

4 New York strip steaks (about 5 ounces each)
¼ cup olive oil
2 teaspoons minced garlic
1 teaspoon salt
½ teaspoon black pepper

1. Place steaks in shallow glass container. Combine oil, garlic, salt and pepper in small bowl; mix well. Pour oil mixture over steaks; turn to coat well. Cover; refrigerate 30 to 60 minutes.

2. Prepare grill for direct cooking.

3. Place steaks on grid. Grill, covered, over medium-high heat 14 minutes for medium (160°F), 20 minutes for well-done (170°F) or according to desired doneness, turning halfway through grilling time.

Makes 4 servings

Jerk
Ribs

Prep Time: 10 minutes • **Cook Time:** 90 minutes

2 pounds pork back ribs
2 tablespoons dried minced onion
4 teaspoons ground thyme
1 tablespoon sugar
1 tablespoon onion powder
2 teaspoons salt
2 teaspoons ground allspice
2 teaspoons black pepper
1 teaspoon ground red pepper
½ teaspoon ground nutmeg
½ teaspoon ground cinnamon

Place all ingredients except ribs in small jar with tight-fitting lid; cover and shake until well blended. Rub dry mixture onto all surfaces of ribs.

Prepare grill with rectangular foil drip pan. Bank briquets on either side of drip pan for indirect cooking. Place ribs on grid over drip pan. Grill on covered grill over low coals 1½ hours or until ribs are tender, turning occasionally. To serve, cut into 1- or 2-rib portions.   *Makes 10 servings*

Conventional Directions: Prepare rub as directed. Roast ribs on rack in shallow pan in 350°F oven for 1½ hours or until ribs are tender.

Favorite recipe from **National Pork Board**

Grilled Sea Bass with
Ripe Olive 'n Caper Salsa (p. 110)

Grilled Red Snapper with
Avocado-Papaya Salsa (p. 116)

**Caribbean Glazed Swordfish
with Grilled Pineapple
Chutney (p. 122)**

**Blackened Catfish
with Creole Vegetables (p. 126)**

Sea & Fire

Spicy Margarita Shrimp

Prep Time: 10 minutes • **Cook Time:** 8 minutes
Marinate Time: 30 minutes

⅔ cup *Frank's*® *RedHot*® *Chile 'n Lime*™ **Hot Sauce**
¼ **cup olive oil**
2 tablespoons lime juice
1 teaspoon grated lime zest
2 teaspoons minced garlic
1½ **pounds jumbo shrimp, shelled and deveined**
1 (16 ounce) jar mild chunky salsa
2 tablespoons minced cilantro
2 red or orange bell peppers, cut into chunks

1. Whisk together *Chile 'n Lime*™ Hot Sauce, oil, lime juice, zest and garlic. Place shrimp into resealable plastic bag. Pour ⅔ cup marinade over shrimp. Seal bag; marinate in refrigerator 30 minutes.

2. Combine remaining marinade with salsa and cilantro in bowl; set aside.

3. Place shrimp and bell pepper chunks on metal skewers. Grill over medium-high direct heat about 8 minutes until shrimp turn pink. Serve with spicy salsa on the side. *Makes 4 to 6 servings*

Tip: To make Mesa Grill BBQ Sauce, add ½ cup **Frank's**® **Redhot**® *Chile 'n Lime*™ Hot Sauce to 1 cup **Cattlemen's**® Authentic Smoke House Barbecue Sauce.

Grilled Sea Bass with Ripe Olive 'n Caper Salsa

1 cup sliced California Ripe Olives
½ cup seeded, diced Roma tomatoes
½ cup chopped oil-packed sun-dried tomatoes
¼ cup minced red onion
¼ cup chopped fresh basil
3 tablespoons capers
2 tablespoons chopped fresh parsley
2 tablespoons Balsamic-style vinaigrette dressing
1 teaspoon minced garlic
8 (6-ounce) sea bass or other white fish fillets
Olive oil

Preheat grill or broiler. Combine all ingredients except sea bass and olive oil in large bowl. Mix well. Adjust seasoning with salt and pepper. Cover and chill. Brush both sides of fillets with olive oil and season with salt and pepper. Broil or grill until fish is firm to the touch, about 5 minutes on each side. Serve each fillet with about ¼ cup of Ripe Olive 'n Caper Salsa.

Makes 8 servings

Favorite recipe from **California Olive Industry**

Caribbean Sea Bass with Mango Salsa

Prep Time: 10 minutes • **Cook Time:** 8 minutes

4 skinless sea bass fillets (4 ounces each), about 1 inch thick
1 teaspoon Caribbean jerk seasoning
Nonstick cooking spray
1 ripe mango, peeled, pitted and diced, *or* 1 cup diced drained bottled mango
2 tablespoons chopped fresh cilantro
2 teaspoons fresh lime juice
1 teaspoon minced jalapeño pepper*

*Jalapeño peppers can sting and irritate the skin, so wear rubber gloves when handling peppers and do not touch your eyes.

1. Prepare grill or preheat broiler. Sprinkle fish with seasoning; coat lightly with cooking spray. Grill fish over medium coals or broil 5 inches from heat 4 to 5 minutes per side or until fish flakes when tested with fork.

2. Meanwhile, combine mango, cilantro, lime juice and jalapeño pepper in small bowl; mix well. Serve salsa over fish.   *Makes 4 servings*

Mustard-Grilled Red Snapper

½ cup Dijon mustard
1 tablespoon red wine vinegar
1 teaspoon ground red pepper
4 red snapper fillets (about 6 ounces each)

1. Spray grid with nonstick cooking spray. Prepare grill for direct cooking.

2. Combine mustard, vinegar and pepper in small bowl; mix well. Coat fish thoroughly with mustard mixture.

3. Place fish on grid. Grill, covered, over medium-high heat 8 minutes without turning until center is opaque.   *Makes 4 servings*

Teriyaki Salmon with Asian Slaw

4 tablespoons reduced-sodium teriyaki sauce, divided
2 (5- to 6-ounce) boneless salmon fillets with skin (1 inch thick)
2½ cups coleslaw mix
1 cup fresh or frozen snow peas, cut lengthwise into thin strips
½ cup thinly sliced radishes
2 tablespoons orange marmalade
1 teaspoon dark sesame oil

1. Prepare grill for direct cooking or preheat broiler. Spoon 2 tablespoons teriyaki sauce over fleshy sides of salmon. Let stand while preparing vegetable mixture.

2. Combine coleslaw mix, snow peas and radishes in large bowl. Combine remaining 2 tablespoons teriyaki sauce, marmalade and sesame oil in small bowl. Add to coleslaw mixture; toss well.

3. Grill salmon, flesh side down, over medium coals or broil salmon 4 to 5 inches from heat source, without turning, 6 to 10 minutes or until center is opaque.

4. Transfer coleslaw mixture to serving plates; top with salmon.

Makes 2 servings

Grilled Red Snapper with Avocado-Papaya Salsa

1 teaspoon ground coriander seeds
1 teaspoon paprika
¾ teaspoon salt
⅛ to ¼ teaspoon ground red pepper
1 tablespoon olive oil
4 skinless red snapper or halibut fish fillets (5 to 7 ounces each)
½ cup diced ripe avocado
½ cup diced ripe papaya
2 tablespoons chopped fresh cilantro
1 tablespoon fresh lime juice
4 lime wedges

1. Prepare grill for direct grilling. Combine coriander, paprika, salt and red pepper in small bowl; mix well.

2. Brush oil over fish. Sprinkle 2½ teaspoons spice mixture over fish fillets; set aside remaining spice mixture. Place fish on oiled grid over medium-hot heat. Grill 5 minutes per side or until fish is opaque.

3. Meanwhile, combine avocado, papaya, cilantro, lime juice and remaining spice mixture in medium bowl; mix well. Serve fish with salsa and garnish with lime wedges. *Makes 4 servings*

Tuna Vera Cruz

3 tablespoons tequila, rum or vodka
2 tablespoons lime juice
2 teaspoons grated lime peel
1 piece (1-inch cube) fresh ginger, minced
2 cloves garlic, minced
1 teaspoon salt
1 teaspoon sugar
½ teaspoon ground cumin
¼ teaspoon ground cinnamon
¼ teaspoon black pepper
1 tablespoon vegetable oil
1½ pounds fresh tuna, halibut, swordfish or shark steaks
Lemon and lime wedges
Fresh rosemary sprigs

Combine tequila, lime juice, lime peel, ginger, garlic, salt, sugar, cumin, cinnamon and pepper in 2-quart glass dish; stir in oil. Add tuna; turn to coat. Cover and refrigerate at least 30 minutes. Remove tuna from marinade; discard marinade. Grill tuna over medium-hot KINGSFORD® Briquets about 4 minutes per side until fish flakes when tested with fork. Garnish with lemon wedges, lime wedges and rosemary sprigs.

Makes 4 servings

Asian Honey-Tea Grilled Prawns

1½ pounds medium raw shrimp, peeled and deveined
Salt
2 green onions, thinly sliced

Marinade
1 cup brewed double-strength orange-spice tea, cooled
¼ cup honey
¼ cup rice vinegar
¼ cup soy sauce
1 tablespoon finely chopped fresh ginger
½ teaspoon ground black pepper

In plastic bag, combine marinade ingredients. Remove ½ cup marinade; set aside for dipping sauce. Add shrimp to marinade in bag, turning to coat. Close bag securely and marinate in refrigerator 30 minutes or up to 12 hours.

Remove shrimp from marinade; discard marinade. Thread shrimp onto 8 skewers, dividing evenly. Grill over medium coals 4 to 6 minutes or until shrimp turn pink and are just firm to the touch, turning once. Season with salt, as desired.

Meanwhile prepare dipping sauce by placing reserved ½ cup marinade in small saucepan. Bring to a boil over medium-high heat. Boil 3 to 5 minutes or until slightly reduced. Stir in green onions.

Makes 4 servings

Favorite recipe from **National Honey Board**

Grilled Salmon Fillets, Asparagus and Onions

Prep and Cook Time: 26 minutes

½ **teaspoon paprika**
6 **salmon fillets (6 to 8 ounces each)**
⅓ **cup bottled honey-Dijon marinade or barbecue sauce**
1 **bunch (about 1 pound) fresh asparagus spears, ends trimmed**
1 **large red or sweet onion, cut into ¼-inch slices**
1 **tablespoon olive oil**
  Salt and black pepper

1. Prepare grill for direct grilling. Sprinkle paprika over salmon fillets. Brush marinade over salmon; let stand at room temperature 15 minutes.

2. Brush asparagus and onion slices with olive oil; season to taste with salt and pepper.

3. Place salmon, skin side down, in center of grid over medium coals. Arrange asparagus spears and onion slices around salmon. Grill salmon and vegetables on covered grill 5 minutes. Turn salmon, asparagus and onion slices. Grill 5 to 6 minutes more or until salmon flakes when tested with a fork and vegetables are crisp-tender. Separate onion slices into rings; arrange over asparagus. *Makes 6 servings*

Caribbean Glazed Swordfish with Grilled Pineapple Chutney

Prep Time: 20 minutes • **Cook Time:** 15 minutes

- ½ cup *Frank's® RedHot®* Cayenne Pepper Sauce or *Frank's® RedHot®* XTRA Hot Cayenne Pepper Sauce
- ¼ cup packed light brown sugar
- 1 teaspoon dried thyme leaves
- ½ teaspoon ground allspice
- 2 tablespoons olive oil
- 4 swordfish steaks, 1-inch thick, seasoned with salt and pepper to taste
- Grilled Pineapple Chutney (recipe follows)

1. Whisk together **Frank's® Redhot®** Sauce, sugar, thyme and allspice. Reserve 3 tablespoons mixture for Grilled Pineapple Chutney.

2. Mix oil into remaining spice mixture; thoroughly baste fish.

3. Place fish on well-greased grill. Cook, covered, over medium-high direct heat for 10 to 15 minutes until opaque in center, turning once. Serve with Grilled Pineapple Chutney.   *Makes 4 servings*

Grilled Pineapple Chutney

- ½ of a fresh pineapple, peeled and sliced ½-inch thick
- 1 red or orange bell pepper, cut into quarters
- 2 tablespoons minced red onion
- 1 tablespoon minced candied ginger
- 1 tablespoon minced cilantro leaves

Grill pineapple and bell pepper about 10 minutes over medium direct heat until lightly charred and tender. Coarsely chop and place in bowl. Add reserved 3 tablespoons hot sauce mixture, onion, ginger and cilantro. Toss to combine.   *Makes 3 cups*

Grilled Tequila Lime Salmon

Prep Time: 5 minutes • **Marinate Time:** 30 minutes
Cook Time: 8 to 10 minutes

1 cup LAWRY'S® Tequila Lime Marinade with Lime Juice, divided
1 pound fresh salmon fillets or steaks
1 lime, cut into wedges (optional garnish)
Fresh cilantro sprigs (optional garnish)

In large resealable plastic bag, combine ¾ cup Tequila Lime Marinade and salmon; seal bag. Marinate in refrigerator for 30 minutes, turning occasionally. Remove salmon from bag, discarding used marinade. Grill salmon until opaque and fish begins to flake easily, for 8 to 10 minutes, brushing often with remaining ¼ cup Marinade. Serve with lime wedges and fresh cilantro for garnish, if desired. *Makes 4 servings*

Meal Idea: Serve with black beans, rice and warm tortillas.

Grilled Garlic-Pepper Shrimp

⅓ cup olive oil
2 tablespoons lemon juice
1 teaspoon garlic pepper blend
20 jumbo shrimp, peeled and deveined
Lemon wedges (optional)

1. Spray grid with nonstick cooking spray. Prepare grill for direct cooking.

2. Meanwhile, combine oil, lemon juice and garlic pepper in large resealable food storage bag; add shrimp. Marinate 20 to 30 minutes in refrigerator, turning bag once.

3. Thread 5 shrimp onto each of 4 skewers;* discard marinade. Grill on grid over medium heat 6 minutes or until pink and opaque. Serve with lemon wedges, if desired. *Makes 4 servings*

*If using wooden skewers, soak in water 20 minutes before using to prevent burning.

Blackened Catfish with Creole Vegetables

Prep Time: 20 minutes • **Cook Time:** 15 minutes

- **⅔ cup *Cattlemen's*® Authentic Smoke House Barbecue Sauce or *Cattlemen's* Award Winning Classic Barbecue Sauce**
- **⅓ cup *Frank's*® RedHot® Chile 'n Lime™ Hot Sauce or *Frank's*® RedHot® Cayenne Pepper Sauce**
- **2 tablespoons Southwest chile seasoning blend or Cajun blend seasoning**
- **1 tablespoon olive oil**
- **4 skinless catfish or sea bass fillets (1½ pounds)**
  Salt and pepper to taste
  Creole Vegetables (recipe follows)

1. Combine barbecue sauce, *Chile 'n Lime*™ Hot Sauce, seasoning blend and oil. Reserve ½ cup mixture for Creole Vegetables.

2. Season fish with salt and pepper to taste. Baste fish with remaining barbecue mixture.

3. Cook fish on a well greased grill over medium direct heat 5 minutes per side until fish is opaque in center, turning once. Serve with Creole Vegetables. *Makes 4 servings*

Creole Vegetables

- **1 red, green or orange bell pepper, cut into quarters**
- **1 large green zucchini or summer squash, cut into pieces**
- **1 large white onion, sliced ½-inch thick**
  Vegetable cooking spray

Arrange vegetables on skewers. Coat vegetables with cooking spray. Grill vegetables over medium direct heat until lightly charred and tender, basting often with reserved ½ cup barbecue sauce mixture.

Makes 4 servings

Pacific Rim Honey-Barbecued Fish

¼ cup honey
¼ cup chopped onion
2 tablespoons lime juice
2 tablespoons soy sauce
2 tablespoons hoisin sauce
2 cloves garlic, minced
1 jalapeño pepper, seeded and minced
1 teaspoon minced fresh gingerroot
4 swordfish steaks or other firm white fish (4 ounces each)

Combine all ingredients except swordfish in small bowl; mix well. Place fish in shallow baking dish; pour marinade over fish. Cover and refrigerate 1 hour. Remove fish from marinade. Grill over medium-hot coals or broil fish about 10 minutes per inch of thickness or until fish turns opaque and flakes easily when tested with fork.   *Makes 4 servings*

Favorite recipe from **National Honey Board**

**Ginger Beef
and Carrot Kabobs (p. 138)**

**Chili-Rubbed
Grilled Vegetable Kabob (p. 144)**

Asian Shrimp
& Steak Kabobs (p. 136)

Sizzling Florida Shrimp (p. 152)

Easy **Kabobs**

Surf & Turf Kabobs

1 pound beef tenderloin, cut into 12 (1¼-inch) chunks
12 jumbo or colossal uncooked shrimp, peeled and deveined, tails on
1 medium onion, cut through core into 12 wedges
1 red or yellow bell pepper, cut into 12 (1-inch) chunks
⅓ cup unsalted butter, melted
3 tablespoons fresh lemon juice
3 cloves garlic, minced
2 teaspoons paprika or smoked paprika
1 teaspoon salt
¼ teaspoon black pepper *or* ground red pepper
Fresh lemon wedges

1. Alternately thread beef, shrimp, onion and bell pepper onto 12-inch-long metal skewers. (Skewer shrimp through ends to form "C" shape for even cooking.)

2. Prepare grill for direct cooking. Combine remaining ingredients, except lemon wedges in small bowl.

3. Place skewers on grid over medium coals; brush with half of butter mixture. Grill 5 minutes; turn and brush with remaining butter sauce. Continue grilling 5 to 6 minutes or until shrimp is opaque (beef will be medium-rare (140°F) to medium doneness). Do not baste during last 5 minutes of grilling. Serve with lemon wedges.   *Makes 4 servings*

Mixed Grill Kabobs

Prep Time: 20 minutes • **Cook Time:** 10 to 15 minutes

1 pound boneless beef sirloin, cut into 1-inch cubes
2 large red, orange or yellow bell peppers, cut into chunks
12 strips bacon, blanched*
12 ounces smoked sausage or kielbasa, cut into ½-inch slices
1 cup red pearl onions, peeled or red onion chunks
1 pound pork tenderloin, cut lengthwise in half; then into
¼-inch wide long strips**
1 cup pineapple wedges
1½ cups *Cattlemen's*® Award Winning Classic Barbecue Sauce

To blanch bacon, place bacon strips into boiling water for 1 minute. Drain thoroughly.
**To easily cut pork, freeze about 30 minutes until very firm.*

1. Arrange beef cubes and 1 bell pepper on metal skewers, weaving bacon strips around all. Place sausage, 1 pepper and onions on separate skewers. Weave strips of pork around pineapple wedges on additional skewers.

2. Baste the different kabobs with some of the barbecue sauce. Cook on a well-greased grill over medium-high direct heat, basting often with remaining barbecue sauce.

3. Serve a trio of kabobs to each person with additional sauce.

Makes 6 to 8 servings

Variation: You may substitute **Cattlemen's**® Authentic Smoke House or Golden Honey Barbecue Sauce.

Asian Shrimp & Steak Kabobs

1 envelope LIPTON® RECIPE SECRETS® Savory Herb with Garlic or Onion Soup Mix
¼ cup soy sauce
¼ cup lemon juice
¼ cup BERTOLLI® Olive Oil
¼ cup honey
½ pound uncooked medium shrimp, peeled and deveined
½ pound boneless sirloin steak, cut into 1-inch cubes
16 cherry tomatoes
2 cups mushroom caps
1 medium green bell pepper, cut into chunks

1. In 13×9-inch glass baking dish, blend savory herb with garlic soup mix, soy sauce, lemon juice, oil and honey; set aside.

2. On skewers, alternately thread shrimp, steak, tomatoes, mushrooms and green pepper. Add prepared skewers to baking dish; turn to coat. Cover and marinate in refrigerator, turning skewers occasionally, at least 2 hours. Remove prepared skewers, reserving marinade.

3. Grill or broil, turning and basting frequently with reserved marinade, until shrimp turn pink and steak is cooked to desired doneness (140°F for rare). Do not brush with marinade during last 5 minutes of cooking.

Makes 8 servings

Menu Suggestion: Serve with corn-on-the-cob, a mixed green salad and grilled garlic bread.

Ginger Beef and Carrot Kabobs

Prep Time: 10 minutes • **Marinate Time:** 4 to 16 hours
Grill Time: 11 to 14 minutes

¾ pound boneless beef top sirloin steak (1 inch thick), cut into 1-inch cubes
¼ cup reduced-sodium soy sauce
1 tablespoon water
1 tablespoon honey
1 teaspoon olive oil
¼ teaspoon ground ginger
¼ teaspoon ground allspice
⅛ teaspoon ground red pepper
1 clove garlic, minced
2 medium carrots, cut into 1-inch pieces (1½ cups)
4 green onions, trimmed to 4-inch pieces

1. Place beef in large resealable food storage bag. Combine soy sauce, water, honey, oil, ginger, allspice, red pepper and garlic in small bowl. Pour over meat in bag. Seal bag; turn to coat meat. Marinate in refrigerator for 4 to 16 hours, turning bag occasionally.

2. Meanwhile, place 1 inch water in medium saucepan. Bring water to a boil. Add carrots. Cover; cook 5 minutes or until crisp-tender. Drain.

3. Prepare grill for direct cooking. Drain meat. Discard marinade. Alternately thread meat and carrot pieces onto 4 skewers.* Add green onion piece to end of each skewer.

4. Grill kabobs over medium coals 11 to 14 minutes or until meat is tender, turning once during grilling. *Makes 4 servings*

*If using wooden skewers, soak in water 20 minutes before using to prevent burning.

Pork and Plum Kabobs

Prep Time: 10 minutes • **Grill Time:** 12 to 14 minutes

¾ pound boneless pork loin chops (1 inch thick), trimmed of fat and cut into 1-inch pieces
1½ teaspoons ground cumin
½ teaspoon ground cinnamon
¼ teaspoon salt
¼ teaspoon garlic powder
¼ teaspoon ground red pepper
¼ cup red raspberry fruit spread
¼ cup sliced green onions
1 tablespoon orange juice
3 plums, pitted and cut into wedges

1. Place pork in large resealable food storage bag. Combine cumin, cinnamon, salt, garlic powder and red pepper in small bowl. Sprinkle over meat in bag. Shake to coat meat with spices.

2. Prepare grill for direct grilling. Combine raspberry spread, green onions and orange juice in small bowl; set aside.

3. Alternately thread pork and plum wedges onto 8 skewers.* Grill kabobs directly over medium heat 12 to 14 minutes or until meat is barely pink in center (155°F), turning once during grilling. Brush frequently with raspberry mixture during last 5 minutes of grilling.   *Makes 4 servings*

*If using wooden skewers, soak in water 20 minutes before using to prevent burning.

Serving Suggestion: A crisp, cool salad makes a great accompaniment to these sweet grilled kabobs.

Beef Kabobs with Apricot Glaze

Prep and Cook Time: 25 minutes

1 can (15¼ ounces) DEL MONTE® Apricot Halves
1 tablespoon cornstarch
1 teaspoon Dijon mustard
½ teaspoon dried basil leaves
1 pound boneless beef top sirloin steak, cut into 1½-inch cubes
1 small green bell pepper, cut into ¾-inch pieces
4 medium mushrooms, cut in half
4 to 8 skewers*

To prevent burning of wooden skewers, soak skewers in water for 10 minutes before assembling kabobs.

1. Drain apricot syrup into small saucepan. Blend in cornstarch until dissolved. Cook over medium heat, stirring constantly, until thickened. Stir in mustard and basil. Set aside.

2. Thread beef, apricots, green pepper and mushrooms alternately onto skewers; brush with apricot syrup mixture. Grill kabobs over hot coals (or broil) about 5 minutes on each side or to desired doneness, brushing occasionally with additional syrup mixture. Garnish, if desired.

Makes 4 servings

Lemon Herbed Seafood Kabobs

2 tablespoons vegetable oil
2 tablespoons finely chopped onion
¼ teaspoon dried rosemary
¼ teaspoon dried thyme leaves
   Grated peel of ½ SUNKIST® lemon
   Juice of 1 SUNKIST® lemon (3 tablespoons)
¼ teaspoon salt
1 pound halibut or shark steak, cut into 1-inch cubes *or*
   1 pound sea scallops (16 to 20)
12 pieces (1 inch square) red or green bell pepper
12 medium button mushrooms

In small nonstick skillet, heat oil; add onion, rosemary, thyme and lemon peel. Cook over low heat 1 to 2 minutes to infuse oil. Remove from heat; add lemon juice and salt. Cool. Pour oil mixture over fish in resealable plastic food storage bag. Seal bag and marinate in refrigerator 1 hour or longer, turning occasionally. To make kabobs, arrange drained fish, bell pepper and mushrooms alternately on four 10-inch metal skewers. Lightly brush mushrooms, peppers and fish with small amount of additional oil. Barbecue on grill 4 to 6 inches above glowing coals or on medium heat of gas barbecue 12 to 14 minutes or until fish is opaque and flakes easily with fork (turning about 3 times). Or, broil 4 inches from heat 12 to 14 minutes. *Makes 4 servings*

Chili-Rubbed Grilled Vegetable Kabobs

2 ears fresh corn, husked
1 medium onion, cut into 12 wedges
1 red bell pepper, cut into 12 (1-inch) chunks
1 yellow bell pepper, cut into 12 (1-inch) chunks
1 green bell pepper, cut into 12 (1-inch) chunks
2 tablespoons olive oil
1 teaspoon seasoned salt
1 teaspoon chili powder
½ teaspoon sugar

1. Cut cobs crosswise into 1-inch pieces. Alternately thread corn, onion and bell peppers onto 12-inch-long metal skewers. Brush oil evenly over vegetables. Combine seasoned salt, chili powder and sugar; sprinkle over both sides of vegetables. Wrap skewers in foil; refrigerate up to 8 hours.

2. Prepare grill for direct cooking. Place unwrapped skewers on grid over medium coals. Grill 10 to 12 minutes or until vegetables are tender, turning occasionally. *Makes 4 servings*

Orange Mustard Ham Kabobs

¾ cup honey mustard barbecue sauce
½ cup orange marmalade
1½ pounds HORMEL® CURE 81® ham, cut into 1-inch cubes
2 small oranges, cut into 6 wedges each

In small bowl, combine barbecue sauce and marmalade; mix well. Remove ½ cup mixture for basting; reserve remaining mixture. Thread ham and orange wedges on skewers. Brush with ½ cup barbecue sauce mixture reserved for basting. Grill over medium-hot coals 10 minutes or until browned, turning frequently and basting with remaining barbecue mixture. Serve with reserved sauce mixture. *Makes 6 servings*

Alternate Method: Orange Mustard Ham Kabobs may be broiled 6 inches from heat source 10 minutes or until browned.

Grilled Chicken Stix

Prep Time: 10 minutes • **Cook Time:** 5 minutes

1 pound thin sliced chicken breast cutlets
12 to 14 wooden skewers, soaked in water
2 oranges, cut into eighths
½ cup barbecue sauce
½ cup honey
3 tablespoons *Frank's® RedHot® Original Cayenne Pepper Sauce*
Spicy Cucumber Salsa (recipe follows)

1. Slice cutlets into ½-inch-wide long strips. Weave strips onto upper half of 8 to 10 skewers. Place skewers into large baking dish. Thread 4 orange pieces each onto remaining 4 skewers. Set aside.

2. Combine barbecue sauce, honey and **Frank's RedHot** Sauce in measuring cup. Reserve ¼ cup sauce for Spicy Cucumber Salsa. Pour ½ cup of remaining mixture over chicken, turning skewers to coat.

3. Grill or broil chicken and orange skewers 5 minutes or until chicken is no longer pink in center and oranges are heated through. Turn and baste often with remaining sauce. Serve with Spicy Cucumber Salsa.

Makes 4 servings

Spicy Cucumber Salsa

Prep Time: 10 minutes

1 large cucumber, peeled, seeded and chopped
1 small red bell pepper, finely chopped
¼ cup finely chopped red onion
2 tablespoons finely chopped fresh cilantro or parsley
Reserved ¼ cup barbecue sauce mixture

1. Combine all ingredients in large bowl; chill. Serve with Grilled Chicken Stix or your favorite grilled chicken or steak recipe.

Makes 4 to 6 servings (about 2 cups)

Chicken Satay

16 chicken tenders (about 2¼ pounds) or 4 boneless, skinless chicken breasts, cut into 16 thin strips
½ cup reduced-sodium soy sauce

Peanut Sauce
1 tablespoon vegetable oil
1 onion, chopped
2 cloves garlic, minced
2 teaspoons ground ginger
½ cup peanut butter
½ cup water
1½ teaspoons ketchup
¼ teaspoon salt
⅛ teaspoon freshly ground black pepper

1. Marinate chicken in soy sauce in large resealable bag 45 minutes.

2. Meanwhile, heat oil in large nonstick skillet over medium-high heat. Add onion and garlic; cook and stir 5 minutes or until golden brown. Add ginger, and stir to blend. Add peanut butter, water, ketchup, salt and pepper, and stir to blend.

3. Reduce heat to low. Cook until peanut sauce is heated through. Transfer to blender and purée until smooth.

4. Spray grid with nonstick cooking spray. Prepare grill for direct cooking. Preheat grill to medium-high heat. Thread chicken strips onto 16 (8-inch) wooden skewers.* Grill chicken over medium-high heat 5 to 6 minutes or until chicken is cooked through.

5. Serve with peanut sauce. *Makes 4 to 6 servings*

When using wooden skewers, soak in water 20 minutes before using to prevent burning.

Fajitas on a Stick

Prep Time: 20 minutes • **Cook Time:** 18 minutes

1¼ pounds boneless, skinless chicken breast halves, cut into 1-inch pieces
1 cup LAWRY'S® Tequila Lime Marinade With Lime Juice
8 wooden skewers, soaked in water for 15 minutes
½ medium onion, sliced into ½-inch slices
½ medium green bell pepper, cut into 1-inch pieces
16 cherry tomatoes
8 MISSION® Flour Tortillas (fajita size), warmed

In large resealable plastic bag, combine chicken and ¾ Lawry's Tequila Lime Marinade With Lime Juice; turn to coat. Close bag and marinate in refrigerator 30 minutes. Remove chicken from Marinade, discarding Marinade.

On wooden skewers, alternately thread chicken, pepper, onion and tomatoes. Grill or broil, brushing frequently with remaining ¼ cup Marinade and turning once, 15 minutes or until chicken is thoroughly cooked.

Remove chicken and vegetables from wooden skewer. Roll-up and serve, if desired, with sour cream and shredded cheddar cheese.

Makes 8 fajitas

Variation: Also great using LAWRY'S® Mesquite Marinade With Lime Juice.

Barbecue Pork Kabobs

½ **cup ketchup**
¼ **cup white vinegar**
¼ **cup vegetable oil**
1 **tablespoon brown sugar**
1 **teaspoon dry mustard**
1 **clove garlic** *or* ½ **teaspoon garlic powder**
½ **teaspoon salt**
½ **teaspoon Worcestershire sauce**
¼ **teaspoon black pepper**
¼ **teaspoon hot pepper sauce (optional)**
4 **boneless pork chops, cut into 1½-inch cubes**
2 **green bell peppers, cut into chunks**
2 **onions, cut into chunks**

1. Combine ketchup, vinegar, oil, brown sugar, dry mustard, garlic, salt, Worcestershire, black pepper and hot pepper sauce, if desired, in large resealable food storage bag; mix well. Reserve ¼ cup marinade for basting. Add pork; seal bag. Marinate in refrigerator at least 1 hour.

2. Remove pork from marinade; discard used marinade. Alternately thread pork, bell peppers and onions onto skewers. Grill or broil skewers 15 to 20 minutes or until pork is barely pink in center, turning once and basting often with reserved ¼ cup marinade. *Do not baste during last 5 minutes of cooking.* Discard any remaining marinade.

Makes 4 servings

Serving Suggestion: Serve over red beans and rice.

Sizzling Florida Shrimp

1½ pounds Florida Shrimp, peeled and deveined
1 cup Florida mushrooms, cut into halves
½ cup Florida red bell pepper pieces (1-inch pieces)
½ cup Florida onion pieces (1-inch pieces)
1 (8.9-ounce) jar lemon pepper sauce or 1 cup barbecue sauce

Arrange shrimp on wooden skewers with mushrooms, red bell pepper and onion. Place skewers in glass dish and cover with sauce, reserving about 2 tablespoons for basting during cooking. Cover and refrigerate for 1 hour. Prepare grill surface by cleaning and coating with oil. Coals are ready when coals are no longer flaming but are covered with gray ash. Place skewers on grill about 6 inches from coals. Grill shrimp for about 3 to 4 minutes on each side, basting with reserved sauce before turning once. Serve with sautéed asparagus and grilled garlic bread.

Makes 4 servings

Favorite recipe from **Florida Department of Agriculture and Consumer Services, Bureau of Seafood and Aquaculture**

Wine & Rosemary Lamb Skewers

1 cup dry red wine
¼ cup olive oil
3 cloves garlic, cut into slivers
1 tablespoon chopped fresh thyme _or_ 1 teaspoon dried thyme, crumbled
1 tablespoon chopped fresh rosemary _or_ 1 teaspoon dried rosemary, crumbled
2 pounds boneless lamb, cut into 1-inch cubes
Salt and black pepper
4 or 5 sprigs fresh rosemary (optional)
Grilled Bread (recipe follows)

Combine wine, oil, garlic, thyme and rosemary in a shallow glass dish or large heavy plastic food storage bag. Add lamb; cover dish or close bag. Marinate lamb in the refrigerator up to 12 hours, turning several times. Remove lamb from marinade; discard marinade. Thread lamb onto 6 long metal skewers. Season to taste with salt and pepper.

Oil hot grid to help prevent sticking. Grill lamb, on a covered grill, over medium KINGSFORD® Briquets, 8 to 12 minutes, turning once or twice. Remove grill cover and throw rosemary onto coals the last 4 to 5 minutes of cooking, if desired. Move skewers to side of grid to keep warm while bread is toasting. Garnish, if desired. _Makes 6 servings_

Grilled Bread

¼ cup olive oil
2 tablespoons red wine vinegar
1 French bread baguette (about 12 inches long), sliced lengthwise, then cut into pieces
Salt and freshly ground black pepper

Mix oil and vinegar in cup; brush over cut surfaces of bread. Season lightly with salt and pepper. Grill bread cut side down, on an uncovered grill, over medium KINGSFORD® Briquets until lightly toasted.

Makes 6 servings

The publisher would like to thank the companies and organizations listed below for the use of their recipes and photographs in this publication.

American Lamb Council

Australian Lamb

California Olive Industry

Del Monte Corporation

Florida Department of Agriculture and Consumer Services, Bureau of Seafood and Aquaculture

The Hidden Valley® Food Products Company

Holland House® is a registered trademark of Mott's, LLP

Hormel Foods, LLC

The Kingsford® Products Co.

Mrs. Dash®

National Honey Board

National Pork Board

National Turkey Federation

Reckitt Benckiser Inc.

Reprinted with permission of Sunkist Growers, Inc. All Rights Reserved.

Unilever

Wisconsin Milk Marketing Board

VOLUME MEASUREMENTS (dry)

$1/8$ teaspoon = 0.5 mL
$1/4$ teaspoon = 1 mL
$1/2$ teaspoon = 2 mL
$3/4$ teaspoon = 4 mL
1 teaspoon = 5 mL
1 tablespoon = 15 mL
2 tablespoons = 30 mL
$1/4$ cup = 60 mL
$1/3$ cup = 75 mL
$1/2$ cup = 125 mL
$2/3$ cup = 150 mL
$3/4$ cup = 175 mL
1 cup = 250 mL
2 cups = 1 pint = 500 mL
3 cups = 750 mL
4 cups = 1 quart = 1 L

VOLUME MEASUREMENTS (fluid)

1 fluid ounce (2 tablespoons) = 30 mL
4 fluid ounces ($1/2$ cup) = 125 mL
8 fluid ounces (1 cup) = 250 mL
12 fluid ounces ($1 1/2$ cups) = 375 mL
16 fluid ounces (2 cups) = 500 mL

WEIGHTS (mass)

$1/2$ ounce = 15 g
1 ounce = 30 g
3 ounces = 90 g
4 ounces = 120 g
8 ounces = 225 g
10 ounces = 285 g
12 ounces = 360 g
16 ounces = 1 pound = 450 g

DIMENSIONS

$1/16$ inch = 2 mm
$1/8$ inch = 3 mm
$1/4$ inch = 6 mm
$1/2$ inch = 1.5 cm
$3/4$ inch = 2 cm
1 inch = 2.5 cm

OVEN TEMPERATURES

250°F = 120°C
275°F = 140°C
300°F = 150°C
325°F = 160°C
350°F = 180°C
375°F = 190°C
400°F = 200°C
425°F = 220°C
450°F = 230°C

BAKING PAN SIZES

Utensil	Size in Inches/Quarts	Metric Volume	Size in Centimeters
Baking or	$8 \times 8 \times 2$	2 L	$20 \times 20 \times 5$
Cake Pan	$9 \times 9 \times 2$	2.5 L	$23 \times 23 \times 5$
(square or	$12 \times 8 \times 2$	3 L	$30 \times 20 \times 5$
rectangular)	$13 \times 9 \times 2$	3.5 L	$33 \times 23 \times 5$
Loaf Pan	$8 \times 4 \times 3$	1.5 L	$20 \times 10 \times 7$
	$9 \times 5 \times 3$	2 L	$23 \times 13 \times 7$
Round Layer	$8 \times 1 1/2$	1.2 L	20×4
Cake Pan	$9 \times 1 1/2$	1.5 L	23×4
Pie Plate	$8 \times 1 1/4$	750 mL	20×3
	$9 \times 1 1/4$	1 L	23×3
Baking Dish	1 quart	1 L	—
or Casserole	$1 1/2$ quart	1.5 L	—
	2 quart	2 L	—